In Search of
Cultural History

THE PHILIP MAURICE DENEKE LECTURE 1967

BY

E. H. GOMBRICH

CLARENDON PRESS · OXFORD

Oxford University Press, Walton Street, Oxford OX2 6DP

OXFORD   LONDON   GLASGOW
NEW YORK   TORONTO   MELBOURNE   WELLINGTON
IBADAN   NAIROBI   DAR ES SALAAM   CAPE TOWN
KUALA LUMPUR   SINGAPORE   JAKARTA   HONG KONG   TOKYO
DELHI   BOMBAY   CALCUTTA   MADRAS   KARACHI

ISBN 0 19 817168 4

REPRODUCED PHOTOLITHO IN GREAT BRITAIN
BY J. W. ARROWSMITH LTD., BRISTOL

Preface

THE publication of a lecture always presents the author with a dilemma which becomes the more intractable the larger the theme he has treated. To fit the discussion of such a theme into the narrow frame of an hour inevitably demands the sacrifice of many tempting topics and a certain sleight of hand in the concealment of all the lacunae of which only the speaker can be fully aware. When the occasion is over his sins of omission once more begin to haunt the author. There is no rational reason why the paragraphs he drafted and then discarded in the interest of brevity should not be restored for the published version. However, he is likely to find that any concession to these clamouring aspirants threatens to disrupt the superficial balance at which he had finally arrived. His text begins to ladder like a stocking and the distressing situation is hard to mend. The only real remedy would be to write a book, and that was not part of the bargain. A compromise has to be found which somehow preserves the text of the lecture and still saves the lecturer's conscience.

The pages in front of the reader are the result of such a compromise. The text of the lecture delivered at Lady Margaret Hall on 19 November, 1967 survives almost intact, but additions have increased its length to more than double its original size. In particular I have allowed myself more quotations from the authors I discussed; the translations are my own. To make up for the inevitable loosening of the structure which goes with the increased length I have introduced subheadings. Moreover I have added a good many bibliographical references which should enable the reader to follow up some of the themes I could hardly touch upon. Bracketed figures in the text refer to this alphabetical list and are followed, where necessary, by indications of the relevant volume and page numbers. The inclusion of a rather disproportionate selection of my own writings was to help me as far as possible to avoid repeating arguments I have presented elsewhere. I should like here to thank Dr. George H. Nadel, editor of *History and Theory*, for drawing my attention to recent discussions of cultural history. Professor R. L. Colie, Professor Philipp Fehl and my son Richard read the manuscript and suggested important improvements.

In Search of
Cultural History

I. THE TERM AND THE THING

A FEW weeks ago I was travelling in a Minicab across London
when the conversation with the driver naturally turned to the
overcrowding of the Metropolis. The driver was inclined to
blame the lack of rival attractions in many provincial towns
which had no theatres and no concert halls. 'I hate the word
culture,' he said, in what I can only describe as a most cultured
voice, 'I hate the word culture, but...' I was glad it was too
dark for him to see me blushing. I am in charge of an Institute
which was founded as *Die Kulturwissenschaftliche Bibliothek
Warburg*. Its founder, Aby Warburg,(22) had been a student of
Karl Lamprecht,(68) the champion of cultural psychology who
was engaged throughout his life in a running fight with those
professional historians who confined their interest to political
history. Both Warburg and Lamprecht looked up in admiration
to the towering figure of Jakob Burckhardt whose central contribution to *Kulturgeschichte* will have to loom large in this
lecture. Thus the rejection of the word 'culture' by English
culture is a frequent cause of embarrassment to me when I am
asked to explain what the Warburg Institute is about. It helps
me little to point out that this rejection is of comparatively
recent date(69) and that even the word *Kulturwissenschaft*
which sounds so quintessentially Teutonic to modern English
ears has a perfectly respectable English counterpart. The first

chapter of Sir Edward Burnett Tylor's pioneering work on *Primitive Culture* of 1871 is headed 'The Science of Culture'.(62)

Not that I have no sympathy for my driver's reluctance to pronounce the word. It had become tainted for him, as for many other sensitive people, by the highmindedness of Matthew Arnold with his eagerness to spread 'sweetness and light' among the benighted,(69) and by the lowmindedness of German propaganda during the First World War which invented a contrast between German *Kultur*, naturally a good thing, profound and strong, and Western civilization, a bad thing, a mere shallow addiction to gadgetry and materialism.(41) I do not propose to waste time on any of these phony distinctions,(38, 51) but I must draw attention to a subtle change in the aura of the word which may soon render my driver's attitude somewhat obsolete. From the usage of anthropologists exemplified by Burnett Tylor the word has spread to social scientists, especially on the other side of the Atlantic.(37, 62) In this sterilized meaning it has come into vogue again in such terms as 'working-class culture' or even C. P. Snow's 'two cultures' of unhappy memory. These are purely descriptive terms, stripped, it is often claimed, of any so-called 'value judgement'.

Human cultures, according to this tradition—which probably can be traced back to Hippolyte Taine—can be studied as bacterial cultures must be studied, without ranking them in order of value.

It is not my purpose here to add yet further 'Notes towards the definition of culture',(8) for I believe that, whether we like the particular term, or prefer another, we all know what it seeks to describe. At least everybody knows this who has ever travelled from one country to another, or even moved from one social circle to another, and has experienced what it means to be confronted by different ways of life, different systems of reference, different scales of value—in short different cultures.

Whenever peoples came into friendly or hostile contact they must have noticed the gulf that separated their own language and habits from those of the others. Naturally what struck observers in such situations was the unexpected feature or custom that contrasted with the norm to which the reporter was used. Whether you read Herodotus, Tacitus or Marco Polo it is always these differences which are singled out for attention. But the experience cuts both ways. The variety of *mores* existing on the globe also provided a welcome topic for the moralist who wanted to hold up a mirror to his own people, and indeed the contrast in cultures becomes an effective device for satirists from Thomas More to Swift, from Montesquieu's *Lettres Persanes* to Sterne's *Sentimental Journey*. By then, of course, the travellers to foreign lands had long been joined by travellers in time, by historians. What motives had they to concern themselves with the conditions of past cultures rather than with events? The claims and contests of the mighty which sent the historian back to old charters and chronicles mainly fed the stream of political and constitutional history, but where traditional privileges and ancient laws came into play, power and custom could not be neatly separated. The search in the muniment room aroused interest in antiquities, particularly in England,(12) just as the interpretation of ancient laws focused attention on the changing conditions of society. It is hardly an accident that the pioneers of cultural as distinct from political history, e.g. Bodin, Vico and Montesquieu, were trained in the law. In addition there were the scholars interested in literary texts that needed an increasing amount of explanatory glosses, the knowledge of material culture (*realia*) cultivated by classical philologists and leading to the systematic study of 'Antiquities'.(45) Last, but not least, there were the ancestors of my own subject, the early historians of art who, like Vasari, spurned the conception of the mere chronicler and concerned themselves with the conditions that favoured the progress of skill.(19) The question itself was not new. It had been debated in the ancient schools of rhetoric where Longinus no less than Tacitus report discussions whether oratory could survive the conditions of democratic freedom that had brought it into being. Artists, in their turn, liked rather to draw attention to the effects of princely bounty and dreamed of Golden Ages of patronage.(18) But Vasari, for instance, was not blind to the importance of competition, and graphically described it in the *Life of Perugino*.

And yet it could be claimed that such interest in the variety of cultural conditions alone would never have led to the emergence of cultural history had it not been for a novel element—the belief in progress, which alone could unify the history of mankind.

At the time when the words 'culture' and 'civilization' made their appearance and spread in the eighteenth century they were indeed terms of value, to be used in contrast to barbarism, savagery or rudeness.(51, 56) The history of civilization or of culture was the history of man's rise from a near animal state to polite society, the cultivation of the arts, the adoption of civilized values and the free exercise of reason. Thus culture could progress, it could also decline and be lost, and history was legitimately concerned with either of these processes. It was thus that Vico in the *Scienza Nuova* and Voltaire in his *Essai sur les Moeurs* had seen the problem, though neither of them used the term *cultura* or *culture*.(68)

In England it was that optimistic view of progress which Professor Butterfield has called the 'Whig Conception of History' that led to the first essays in this genre, notably William Roscoe's *Life of Lorenzo di Medici* of 1795 which is really a cultural history of Medicean Florence in the early Renaissance. The same tradition was carried forward by the great Macaulay, whose famous chapter in *The History of England* on the condition of the country in 1685 is explicitly intended to bring home to the reader in 1849 the extent of the improvements which had been achieved in the intervening period.

But in a sense it was precisely this optimistic interpretation which led to a demand for a distinction between 'civilization' and 'culture'. For was it really true that all aspects of civilized life advanced together? Was it true that the arts, the sciences, goodness of manners and goodness of heart all kept pace in the process of civilization? There are implicit doubts in Vico and explicit ones in Rousseau. The very concern of the eighteenth century with the enlightenment, the creation of conditions favouring culture, also led to an increasing interest in the cultural conditions of the past. Winckelmann's praise for the arts of Greece went with a conviction that the whole of Greek civilization accounted for this efflorescence. His conclusion was that this made ancient civilization supreme, the model to which all others should aspire. It was easy, however, to turn the tables on these cultural expatriates and to point out to them that on their own reasoning these conditions could never come back. If art is embedded in culture we must accept that different cultures produce different arts. The Northern climate and the Christian religion both make it inopportune to build temples, but then the new conditions created a new flower in the Gothic cathedral. It was of course Herder, above all, who argued along these lines, and who therefore rejected the idea of a scale of excellence by which you could measure culture. Not that he was a complete relativist. He still held fast to the idea of a divine plan which led mankind towards *Humanität*, but since history reflects such a grand design it would be arrogant to disregard the earlier stages; how could we, indeed, when God had manifested Himself among the Hebrew shepherds?

These sentiments, scattered about in the prolix and humane writings of Herder, were transposed into a metaphysical

system claiming the necessary truth of logic by Georg Friedrich
Hegel.

II. THE HEGELIAN SYSTEM

Some people are allergic to Hegel and I confess that my own
tolerance is low. But I do not want here to repeat what Schopen-
hauer, Bertrand Russell (59) and my friend Sir Karl Popper(52,
54) have said with much greater authority; even less do I want
to argue against those who may have been provoked by these
denunciations into a defence of Hegel.(11, 44) What I want to
explain is merely why we are today in search of cultural history.(1, 5, 15, 16, 58) We are in search, I shall maintain, because
Kulturgeschichte has been built, knowingly and unknowingly,
on Hegelian foundations which have crumbled.

It is well known that Hegel wanted to build these foundations on a metaphysical system which he claimed to have
developed out of Kant's critiques of metaphysics. But what is
more relevant for the present context is rather Hegel's return
to the traditions of theology. Admittedly his theology would
have to be classed as heretical for it disregards the Christian
dogma of the creation as a one-time event and that of the incarnation as an equally unique occurrence in time. The history
of the universe was for Hegel the history of God creating Himself and the history of mankind was in the same sense the continuous Incarnation of the Spirit.

In his book on *The Great Chain of Being* (1936) Arthur Lovejoy has described how, in the course of the eighteenth century,
the new idea of Progress had gradually been fused with the
old image of a hieratic universe. The ladder of existence from
stones to plants, from plants to animals upwards to man and
hence through the spiritual realm of the angelic orders to the
divine apex was no longer conceived as static and immutable.

There is a process of ascent along these rungs of the ladder leading the creation towards a divine culmination. Hegel translated this ascent into the terms of logical categories and thus turned the cosmic process into the progression of the divine spirit thinking itself, impelled by the need of resolving contradictions to move to a higher and higher plane of articulation. Human history, the rise of civilization, is part of this progress, indeed it repeats its essential and inevitable dialectical steps as an ascent through the logical categories till the divine at last comes to self-awareness in the mind of Herr Professor Hegel.

I know that this particular conclusion has been denied, but it certainly is part of Hegel's conception of History as an unfolding of divine reasoning that whatever is must also be right, right because meaningful as a step towards the self-realization of the spirit.

It is clear that within this system the contrast between the idea of culture as a term of value and its use as a merely descriptive word has no place; it is 'resolved', as Hegelians would say, on the higher plane on which every culture is right as a necessary stage. One does not argue with the Absolute. This applies not only to the past but also to the present. The critic can watch the signs of the times, he has no right to judge them. Every person can hope to be the mouthpiece, indeed almost the incarnation, of the spirit. Hegel called Napoleon 'the world spirit on horseback' and Gertrude Stein claimed to be the embodiment of the *Zeitgeist*. But in a sense everything is, at least everything and everybody can become, an instrument of the spirit. The invention of gunpowder in Hegel's view was such a manifestation of the divine. 'Mankind needed it, and lo, it was there.' The need arose because the feudal system had to be dissolved and, strange though we may find this, the invention led war on to a higher, because a more abstract, plane. Killing became more anonymous and so did courage (29, p. 508).

And yet, I want to maintain, this rather blasphemous and heretical interpretation is an extension, or possibly a perversion, of the Christian interpretation of providential history. Both in the Judaic and in the Christian tradition history was seen as part of a divine plan in which the actions of people and of nations were conceived as manifestations of the divine will. Not only the history of the Chosen People but even that of the Roman conquerors was so interpreted because the Plan of Salvation could only come into effect in 'the fullness of time' when the oecumene was sufficiently united by a common language to be ripe for the good news of the Incarnation.(13, 64) From then on, of course, history is the stage for the battle between the militant Church and the adversary; but the outcome of that fight is assured with the Second Coming, announced by tremendous portents, when history as we know it will come to an end. The medieval abbot Joachim of Fiore had made these prophecies more specific and worked out a trinitarian system of history in which the Old Testament represented the realm of the Father, the Christian era the realm of the Son, which would in turn be replaced very soon by the third realm—*das dritte Reich*—the era of the Spirit.

The fateful expression to which I have just alluded reminds us of the spell which these chiliastic hopes exerted on successive interpreters of history. Lessing had referred to the visions of the abbot,(42) and similar mystical and especially Trinitarian speculations also played their part in Hegel's early development.(66, 28, 27) The degree to which these influences left their mark on his *Lectures on the Philosophy of History* still remains to be examined. Consider especially the pages in which he deals with the coming of Christ when, as he puts it,

the identity of the subject and of God comes into the world in the fullness of time, the awareness of this identity is the recognition of God in His truth (29, p. 415).

Not surprisingly, perhaps, it is the Germanic peoples who are the instrument and the vessel of the new Spirit which unfolds in three phases, that of the conquest of the Roman world, that of the feudal monarchy of the Middle Ages and finally in the phase initiated by the Reformation. 'These three,' we read, 'may be described as the realm of the Father, the Son and the Holy Ghost' (29, pp. 441–2). The same succession, he says in retrospect, can also be found in the pre-Christian stage of history where the Persians are thought by Hegel to represent the Father, the Greeks the Son and the Romans the Holy Ghost, each of course on a correspondingly lower plane.

Every one of these peoples, as we have seen, embodied a necessary phase of the ascending spirit; their individual spirit, their *Volksgeist*, was a temporary form of the absolute Spirit on its path through history. For this is the decisive aspect of Hegel's position for my purpose. Here are his own words as they were recorded by students who attended his course on the philosophy of history:

World history represents . . . the evolution of the awareness of the spirit of its own freedom. . . . Every step, being different from every other one, has its own determined and peculiar principle. In history such a principle becomes the determination of the spirit—a peculiar national spirit (*ein besonderer Volksgeist*). It is here that it expresses concretely all the aspects of its consciousness and will, its total reality; it is this that imparts a common stamp to its religion, its political constitution, its social ethics, its legal system, its customs but also to its science, its art and its technical skills. These particular individual qualities must be understood as deriving from that general peculiarity, the particular principle of a nation. Conversely it is from the factual details present in history that the general character of this peculiarity has to be derived (29, pp. 101–2).

I like to picture the content of this all-important paragraph diagrammatically as a wheel from the hub of which there radiate eight spokes. These spokes represent the various concrete manifestations of the national Spirit, in Hegel's words 'all the aspects of its consciousness and will'. They are the nation's religion, constitution, morality, law, customs, science, art, and technology. These manifestations which are visible on the periphery of my wheel must all be understood in their individual character as the realizations of the *Volksgeist*. They all point to a common centre. In other words, from whichever part on the outside of the wheel you start moving inwards in search of their essence, you must ultimately come to the same central point. If you do not, if the science of a people appears to you to manifest a different principle from that manifested in its legal system, you must have lost your way somewhere.

Hegel admits that you can only practise this art when you are familiar with the *a priori* knowledge deduced from his system, but he claims that the same is true of astronomers like Kepler, who must be familiar with the *a priori* laws of geometry to discover the cosmic laws of motion. The comparison is clearly misleading and I should like to replace it by another. Hegel's historian practises exegetics. His *a priori* knowledge is less like that of an astronomer than like that of a devout interpreter of the Scriptures who knows, for instance, that every event described in the Old Testament can be interpreted as foreshadowing another event described in the Gospels. The Jews crossing the Red Sea are a type for the anti-type of Christ's Baptism, Melchisedek offering Abraham bread and wine signifies the Eucharist. For God did not only reveal His plan through the mouth of the prophets, but also in ordering the events themselves.

I have given an example of this exegetic technique in Hegel's interpretation of the invention of gunpowder. I can only point briefly to one more, his interpretation of the Grand Sphinx of

Egypt. The sphinx, we read, can be seen as a symbol of the Egyptian spirit, the human head looking out of the animal body represents the spirit beginning to raise itself from the fetters of nature without however liberating itself fully. And just as the ingenuities of the allegorical interpretations of the Scriptures often compel admiration, so does Hegel's skill in representing every aspect of ancient Egyptian civilization in the light of this preconceived notion: Egyptian writing is still hieroglyphic, based on the sensuous image, not on abstract letters, Egyptian religion worships animals because the dim and inert spirit of the Egyptians cannot rise to a higher idea, and though the Egyptians were the first to believe in immortality they still clung to the body, the mummy.

Not all of Hegel's interpretations look as forced and Procrustean as his reading of Egyptian culture. On the contrary, his skill in imposing his scheme on a variety of cultural events must have been considerable if we are to explain the hold which his reading of history maintained on subsequent generations. His pages on the 'Dissolution of the Middle Ages through art and science' are a case in point. He sees the Renaissance in Herder's terms as 'a soaring of the spirit towards a higher humanity' (29, p. 515).

The Grave, Death ... and the Beyond have been given up. The principle of here and now that drove the world to the crusades developed into a worldliness for its own sake. ... But the Church remained and held on to externals. However, it so fell out, that this externalization did not remain crude, for it was transfigured by art. Art vivifies and animates ... the merely sensual and imbues it with form which expresses the soul, the sentiment, the spirit. ... (p. 515)

There is a great difference whether the mind is confronted by a mere thing such as the Eucharist or any stone, wood or crude image, or is contemplating a profound painting, a beautiful work of sculpture where soul relates to soul and spirit to spirit. In the first instance the spirit is . . . tied to something totally other which is sensuous and not spiritual. Here, however, the sensual is also beautiful, the spiritual form that animates it, is also true. . . . (p. 515)

Yet in this way art transcended the principle of the Church. Being confined to sensuous representations it was at first still considered to be safe. Hence the Church still accepted art, but became dissociated from the free spirit that had created art, when that spirit had risen to the realms of thought and of science. . . . (p. 516)

For art was assisted and uplifted by the study of antiquity (the name *humaniora* is very significant, for in these works of antiquity humanity and human education are honoured) . . . scholastic formalism was replaced by a very different content: Plato became known in the West and with him there arose a new world of man. . . . (pp 516/17)

The third main trend to be mentioned is the outward urge of the spirit, man's desire to get to know his earth . . . the new technical means of the marine compass assisted shipping . . . the means are found when the demand exists.

These three facts, the so-called revival of learning, the efflorescence of the fine arts and the discovery of America . . . may be compared to the dawn, the harbinger of a new fine day after the long, fateful and terrible night of the Middle Ages. . . . (p. 518)

In Hegel's system this dawn announces the great 'all-transfiguring sunrise' of the Reformation, the modern age in the description of which he lets his Theodicy culminate.

The interpretations of cultural history in these Lectures on the Philosophy of History are supplemented and partly expanded in Hegel's lectures on Aesthetics, in which he displayed much skill and even poetic gift in presenting the development of the arts as a logical process accompanying and reflecting the unfolding of the spirit. The whole system of the arts is here turned into a temporal hierarchy, beginning with architecture, the most 'material' of the arts, first appearing in the huge lumps of the pyramids, progressing to sculpture which of course finds its apogee in Greece, and then to the even more spiritual, dematerialized medium of painting which, in Hegel's view, corresponds to the Christian Age of Faith. But painting, in its turn, tends increasingly towards the less tangible art of music which must yield its place to poetry as even closer to pure thought. It is well known that Hegel believed that poetry, too, would be dissolved when the Spirit would no longer need images for its manifestation but would turn into abstract philosophy.

Whatever the validity of these individual interpretations, which are frequently presented with great persuasiveness, it was the technique itself which exerted a tremendous appeal. Those who accepted Hegel's logic now had the proof of what had before been a mere matter of intuition, the feeling that each art and each culture existed in its own right and could not be judged by other standards; and yet this proof did not invalidate the equally intuitive conviction that the history of civilization was and remained a history of growing values, a history of progress.

No type of historian has a greater stake in this approach than the historian of art. Indeed it might be claimed that a history, as distinct from a critical evaluation, of the art of the past only became possible in the light of this interpretation. For Vasari as for Winckelmann, art had indeed responded to favourable conditions but declined when conditions altered. Now there was no decline, only the logical progression of the *Zeitgeist* which had brought about changes in the monuments of the past. The changing styles of art thus became the index of the changing spirit. The Hegelian creed was formulated in the introduction of 1843 of a history of art by the now largely forgotten German art historian Carl Schnaase:(60)

Art, too, belongs to the necessary expressions of mankind; indeed one may say that the genius of mankind expresses itself more completely and more characteristically in art than in religion. (p. 83)

It is true that the keen eye of the beholder will also penetrate deep into the nature of a nation when examining its political life or its scientific achievement, but the most subtle and most characteristic features of a people's soul can only be recognized in its artistic creations. (p. 86)

Thus the art of every period is both the most complete and the most reliable expression of the national spirit in question, it is something like a hieroglyph ... in which the secret essence of the nation declares itself, condensed, it is true, dark at first sight, but completely and unambiguously to those who can read these signs ... thus a continuous history of art provides the spectacle of the progressive evolution of the human spirit. . . . (p. 87)

III. BURCKHARDT'S HEGELIANISM

The historian who vindicated the approach to *Kulturgeschichte* through art in the eyes of the nineteenth century was of course not Schnaase but Jacob Burckhardt. It may appear outrageous to rank Burckhardt among the Hegelians, since he often expressed his dislike of Hegel's brand of philosophy. He always stressed that he distrusted systems and believed in facts. But I hope to show that Burckhardt here illustrates the important methodological truth that it is precisely those people who want to discard all 'preconceived' theories who are most likely unconsciously to succumb to their power. There is no more striking example of this truth than a letter which Burckhardt wrote at the age of twenty-four to his friend Karl Fresenius. It must therefore be quoted at some length:

You have become a philosopher, and yet you will have to concede to me the following—a person such as myself who is quite unsuited to speculative theorizing and who never, even for a minute in a whole year, feels disposed towards abstract thought, such a person will do best if he attempts to approach the higher questions of life and of research in his own way and tries to clarify these issues as best he can. My own substitute, then, is my effort to achieve with every day a more intense immediacy in the perception of essentials. By nature I cling to the tangible, to visible reality and to history. But I have a bent for incessantly looking for parallels in co-ordinating facts and have thus succeeded on my own in arriving at a few generalized principles. I am aware of the fact that there exists a yet higher principle of generality soaring above these multifarious principles and, maybe, I shall be able to rise towards that level. You cannot imagine to what an extent this effort, however one-sided it may be, gradually lends significance to the facts of history, the works of art, the monuments of all ages, as witnesses of earlier phases in the evolution of the Spirit. Believe me, I often feel an awesome thrill when I see this age clearly present in ages past. The highest goal of human history, the development of the spirit towards free-dom, has become my ruling conviction, and so my studies cannot betray me and cannot let me go under, but remain my tutelary guiding light as long as I live. (3, 1, 206f.)

Though Burckhardt believed that he was generalizing from the observed facts of history, what he ultimately found in the facts was the Hegelian world spirit he had rejected as a specu-lative abstraction. It is true that he was not entirely unaware of this situation. He admits a few lines later in the letter that though the speculations of another man could never console or help him, he is still affected by them since they are part of the spirit which dominates the intellectual atmosphere of the nine-teenth century.

Indeed, it may well be that I am unconsciously guided by some of the threads of recent philosophy. But allow me to remain on this humble level, let me sense and feel history rather than understand it through its first principles. (Ibid.)

However, he promised he would read Hegel, and no doubt he did.

In his important introduction to Burckhardt's *Griechische Kulturgeschichte* Professor Momigliano has shown some of the

links which connect even that series of lectures from Burckhardt's later years with the philosophical preoccupation of
Romanticism.(46) He has in particular pointed to the influence
of one of Burckhardt's teachers, the classical scholar A. Boeckh,
in whose writings the idea of a *Volksgeist* plays a central
part.(67) Nor is the evidence lacking that the idea of the
Zeitgeist was accepted by the young Burckhardt as a matter of
course. In a letter to his friend Kinkel, who wanted to write
on the arts of the Netherlands, he writes: 'Conceive your task
as follows: How does the spirit of the fifteenth century express
itself in painting? Then everything becomes simple.' (4 May
1847) (3, III, p. 70).

It has often been deplored that Burckhardt never came to
write such a history of art himself. In his first book on cultural
history, *The Age of Constantine the Great* (1853), art plays
indeed a rather subordinate role. Clearly Burckhardt here tried
to realize his ideal of a history based on *Anschauung*, immediacy. He aims at narration, quotation and depiction with little
overt interpretation. Perhaps the subject of the book was
especially favourable to this approach. The position of Constantine's reign as a turning point in history is so profoundly established in the reader's mind that the general framework is all
but given—we look for signs of declining paganism and of the
rise of the new age, and the historian hardly has to sketch in the
context more firmly than Burckhardt did.

No doubt Burckhardt thought the same of that other age of
transition to which he turned, the age of the Renaissance to
which he devoted his most famous masterpiece, *Die Kultur der
Renaissance in Italien* of 1860 (2, v). But here it must be appar-
ent to every reader that Burckhardt saw that civilization
through the medium of its art.

He had begun his studies as a lover of Northern medieval
art, but had experienced a kind of conversion on his Italian

journeys. The outcome of this conversion had been his *Cicerone* of 1855, subtitled 'a guide to the enjoyment of works of art in Italy'.

There is also very little room for theory in this perceptive guide-book, but it is naturally pervaded by the interpretation of Renaissance art that had become commonplace by the middle of the nineteenth century and is still in evidence, I mean the contrast between the spirituality of the Age of Faith and the sensuality of the subsequent age. It was a polarity that had been created by the Romantics and used, of course, by Hegel. We have seen that for him the revival of the arts with their attention to the external world was one of the factors in the disintegration of the Middle Ages. The few but eloquent lines which Burckhardt devoted in the *Cicerone* to the 'New Spirit' that came over sculpture and painting in the fifteenth century conform to this conception of the Age.

The generalized facial types are now replaced by individualities, the former system of expressions, gestures and draperies is replaced by an infinitely rich truth to life.... Beauty, formerly ... the highest attribute of Holiness ... now yields to ... clarity ... However, where it still comes into existence, it is a newborn sensuous beauty which asks for its undiminished portion of what is earthly and real.... (2, IV, p. 186)

Like Hegel, Burckhardt was convinced that this 'new spirit' transcended and therefore contradicted the demands of the Church. These demands, he suggests, are largely negative. The spirit of worship must not be deflected and diverted by anything that reminded the beholder of the realities of secular life. Wherever these are deliberately brought into art the picture will no longer look devout.

The lines of approach were therefore staked out before Burckhardt began to think of a book on the whole of the

Civilization of the Renaissance. It may seem surprising that this work ultimately lacked a chapter on art, and Burckhardt himself referred to this *lacuna*. It is hard, however, to imagine how he could have made good this omission without repeating much of what he had written in the *Cicerone*.

We know something about Burckhardt's working methods during the four years in which he prepared *Die Kultur der Renaissance in Italien*. He obviously knew what he was looking for. He mentions (3, IV, p. 30) for instance that he collected seven hundred excerpts from Vasari's *Lives*, cutting up his notebooks in little slips for use in the appropriate places. There must have been similar numbers of slips from other texts of the period such as Vespasiano's *Memoirs* or Benvenuto Cellini's *Autobiography*, but what is impressive in the long run is not the number of sources he managed to read and excerpt, but rather his economy in their use, and the magic touch with which he turned these selected extracts into signs of the time.

In my youth the book was still a classic in German-speaking countries, and that meant that it was read by quite a large number of people as providing a passport to *Bildung*, to 'culture' in the Victorian sense of the term. Many may have found it a bit hard going, but they must also have enjoyed the wealth of memorable detail, the concise pen portraits of *condottieri* and of humanists, the tersely told anecdotes about vendettas and practical jokes, the quotations from poets and historians revealing their attitudes to subjects as diverse as scenery, honour or death. The villainies, the gaieties, the feats of prowess, the craving for fame, all this formed part of the panorama that was *Die Kultur der Renaissance*. It was with these scenes and incidents that countless travellers to Italy peopled the streets of Florence, Siena and Venice in their imagination.

Nobody can accuse Burckhardt of having failed to warn his readers that his criteria of selection and arrangement were subjective. He said so in the very first paragraph of the book which he calls a mere essay in the original sense of the term:

> The outlines of a cultural period and its mentality may present a different picture to every beholder and the same studies which resulted in this book might easily have led others to essentially different conclusions.

But though Burckhardt was fully aware of the part interpretation plays in any such enterprise, neither he himself nor, as far as I know, any of his subsequent commentators seems to have realized to what an extent his interpretation was guided by Hegel's theory of history.(36, 10)

There must be a psychological reason for this reluctance, on the part of German-speaking critics, to show up this connexion. One feels in good company in attacking Hegel; but to criticize the intellectual foundation of Burckhardt's work is a different matter. He is the father figure of cultural history whose very tone of voice carries authority. I feel that my own hand trembles a little as I am setting out to sacrifice and dissect a work that has so largely inspired the founder of the Warburg Institute.

The heart of the book, the main thesis, is expressed in the famous paragraph in which Burckhardt contrasts the mentality of the Renaissance with that of the Middle Ages:

> In the Middle Ages both sides of human consciousness—that which faces the outside world and that which is turned towards man's inner life—lay dreaming or only half-awake, as if they were covered by a common veil, a veil woven of faith, delusion and childish dependence. Seen across this veil reality and history appeared in the strangest colours, while man was only aware of himself in universal categories such as race, nation, party, guild or family. It was in Italy that this veil was first blown away and that there awoke an objective attitude towards the state and towards all the things of this world while, on the other side, subjectivity emerged with full

force so that man became a true individual mind and recognized himself as such. (p. 95)

One does not need to know Hegel well to recognize in these polarities some of his favourite categories. There is a constant play in Hegel with the inward and outward turning of the spirit, and with its movement from the general to the particular. Remembering Hegel's thesis that the Trinitarian or tripartite divisions of the Christian era repeat on a higher plane the evolution of the spirit from Persia to Greece and from Greece to Rome, it becomes even more significant that in Hegel the general principle of Roman history (which corresponds to the Renaissance) is due to the inward movement of the spirit producing *subjektive Innerlichkeit* which leads to the juridical idea of an abstract personality manifested in private property. It is this generalized subjectivity which remains the ruling principle of the Germanic peoples, but in the third phase, which ends the Middle Ages, the objective spirit can arise when the subjective free spirit determines to adhere to form.

One must be grateful to Burckhardt for having kept this scaffolding largely out of sight, but the basic Hegelian assumption is not concealed:

Every cultural epoch which presents itself as a complete and articulate whole expresses itself not only in the life of the state, in religion, art and science, but also imparts its individual character to social life as such. (p. 257)

As to the state, this individual character is summed up by Burckhardt in his famous opening chapter entitled 'The State as a Work of Art' (*Der Staat als Kunstwerk*). This curious notion, which has been much debated, becomes immediately intelligible when you remember that the third chapter in Hegel's section on the Greeks is headed *Das politische Kunstwerk* ('The Political Work of Art'), a chapter, by the way, which is preceded by one on the shaping of the 'beautiful individuality'.

Like Hegel, Burckhardt sees the progression of the spirit as an inevitable process, and like him he sees it embodied in successive national spirits. Hence his rejection of the conventional idea that the Renaissance is to be equated with the revival of Antiquity.

> The Renaissance would not have been that exalted world historical necessity it was, if that revival could be ignored. Yet it is one of the main tenets of this book, on which we must insist, that it was not this revival alone, but its close alliance with an independently existing Italian national spirit that achieved the conquest of the Western world. (p. 124)

Given this necessity Burckhardt had little patience with the Romantics who regretted the passing of the Middle Ages; one does not argue with the Absolute:

> It is certainly true that many a noble flower tends to perish in such a large process ... but one should not therefore wish that the great universal event had never happened. (p 124)

For ultimately the process of which the Renaissance formed part is progress. It is true that Burckhardt, later in his life, increasingly moved away from an optimistic interpretation of history. But in his book of 1860 he not only adopted the formula about the discovery of man and the world into which Michelet had so skilfully distilled the gist of Hegel's interpretation; he also opened his presentation on a note of Hegelian optimism:

> Freed from the countless barriers which elsewhere impeded progress, developed into a higher degree of individuality, and schooled by Classical Antiquity, the Italian spirit turned towards the discovery of the external world and its representation in language and in art. (p. 202)

The breaking down of barriers and the new objectivity were really two sides of the same coin. The new realism in art and the objective approach to politics exemplified in Machiavelli, the egotism of rulers and the breakdown of conventional morality on which Burckhardt sometimes dwells with suspicious relish, are represented as inseparable. Others, including Macauley, had emphasized before him that the freedom and moral licence of the period went together. But Burckhardt was anxious to eliminate all vestiges of condemnation. The evolution towards egotism was not the fault of Renaissance man; it was imposed by a verdict of world history, '*ein weltgeschichtlicher Ratschluss*', which ultimately all Europe had to obey.

In itself it is neither good nor evil ... it was the Italian of the Renaissance however who had to withstand the first tremendous surge of the new age. (p. 329)

I hope these quotations will suffice to show that Burckhardt's picture of the Italian Renaissance was painted in a Hegelian frame. But I might be accused of special pleading if I omitted to mention a remark in which he dissociates himself from one of Hegel's tenets, the role assigned to the Reformation in the evolution of the Spirit. Burckhardt raises the question of why the Italian Renaissance with its opposition to the medieval Church, had not achieved the Reformation, why Italy had remained Catholic while Germany went Protestant. His answer does not question the fundamental truth of Hegelian determinism but introduces a note of warning against its dogmatism.

Such tremendous events as the Reformation of the sixteenth century may altogether elude all the deductions of the philosophers of history, as far as the details of their origin and their development are concerned, *however clearly it may be possible to prove their necessity in general outlines* (my italics). The movements of the spirit, their sudden flashes, their extensions and their interruptions remain a mystery, at least to our eyes, since we can never see more than just a few of the sources at work. (p. 330)

It is certainly no accident that this mild caution occurs in connexion with the problem of the Reformation. For in this respect Burckhardt did indeed interpret the plot of history differently from Hegel. To the Berlin professor the Reformation was almost the consummation of the entire historical process; it assured the hegemony of the Germanic nations and of Prussia, leaving behind the Catholic South, which had emancipated itself from the Church without being able to get rid of it. Burckhardt, who had begun his career as a student of theology only to abandon it for history, conceived of the development in terms of the growth of a new non-Christian *Weltanschauung*, the philosophy of the modern world.

It is in this light that we must read the concluding pages of the *Civilization of the Renaissance*, in which Burckhardt attempts to penetrate to the core of the period, which he finds in the Neo-Platonic revival of Lorenzo's circle.

In the hymns of Lorenzo, which we are tempted to call the most sublime expression of the spirit of that school, theism is expressed without reservations, a theism grounded on the striving to see the world as a great moral and physical *cosmos*.

While the men of the Middle Ages regarded the world as a vale of tears . . . there arose here, in the circle of elect spirits, the conception of the visible world as a creation by God through Love . . . of which He would remain the continuous Mover and Incessant Creator (*dauernder Beweger und Fortschöpfer*).

Echoes of medieval mysticism here link up with Platonic doctrines and with a peculiarly modern spirit. Perhaps it was here that there ripened an ultimate fruit of that discovery of the world and of man for the sake of which alone the Renaissance in Italy must be called the leader and guide of our Epoch. (pp. 405–6)

Behind the reticence of this ending we can discern an avowal of Burckhardt's own faith in a God who continues to create in and through history, and this faith he never abandoned, however much he dissociated himself from the Hegelian progressivism of the nineteenth century.(40) Whether it was also the faith of Lorenzo de' Medici is of course an entirely different question. We are no longer under the Hegelian compulsion to find in all aspects of the Renaissance an adumbration of the Modern World.

Not that we should reproach Burckhardt for having built his picture of the period around a 'preconceived idea'. Without such an idea history could never be written at all. The infinite array of documents and monuments which the past has bequeathed to us cannot be grasped without some principle of relevance, some theory which brings order into the atomic facts as the magnet creates a configuration out of inert iron filings.

It is the secret of Burckhardt's strength that he built his masterpiece round a theory. Had he not done so the book would not have remained for a century the focus of discussion about the Renaissance.(10, 14, 30) There is hardly a single trait in his picture of the period which somebody or other has not wished to revise for good reasons, but few even of his critics have acknowledged the all-important fact that the picture is too consistent for such piecemeal alterations. If it does not stand up to a fresh reading of the evidence we cannot tamper with the image here or there. We must examine the methodological armature around which it was built. This armature is the Hegelian construct of cultural history with its corollary, the 'exegetic method'. Postulating the unity of all manifestations of a civilization, the method consists in taking various elements of culture, say Greek architecture and Greek philosophy, and asking how they can be shown to be the expression of the same

Certainly this "method" underlies undergraduate interdisciplinary studies. Indeed, it underlies "liberal arts"

spirit.(46) The end of such an interpretation must always be a triumphant Euclidian Q.E.D., since Hegel had bequeathed to the historian that very task: to find in every factual detail the general principle that underlies it.

IV. HEGELIANISM WITHOUT METAPHYSICS

Thus it is quite consistent that Burckhardt's successor in Basel, the great art historian Heinrich Wölfflin, writes in his first book, in *Renaissance and Baroque* of 1888:

To *explain* a style cannot mean anything but to fit its expressive character into the general history of the period, to prove that its forms do not say anything in their language that is not also said by the other organs of the age. (71, p. 58)

Wölfflin was never quite at ease with this formula(20) but it still dominated his work and that of others. Not that Hegelian metaphysics were accepted in all their abstruse ramifications by any of these historians any more than they were by Burckhardt. The point is rather that all of them felt, consciously or unconsciously, that if they let go of the magnet that created the pattern, the atoms of past cultures would again fall back into random dustheaps.

In this respect the cultural historian was much worse off than any other historian. His colleagues working on political or economic history had at least a criterion of relevance in their restricted subject-matter. They could trace the history of the reform of Parliament, of Anglo-Irish relations, without explicit reference to an all-embracing philosophy of history. But the history of culture as such, the history of all the aspects of life as it was lived in the past, could never be undertaken without some ordering principle, some centre from which the panorama can be surveyed, some hub on which the wheel of Hegel's diagram can be pivoted. Thus the subsequent history of historiography of culture can perhaps best be interpreted as a succession of attempts to salvage the Hegelian assumption without accepting Hegelian metaphysics. This was precisely what Marxism claimed it was doing. The Hegelian diagram was more or less maintained, but the centre was occupied not by the spirit but by the changing conditions of production. What we see in the periphery of the diagram represents the superstructure in which the material conditions manifest themselves. Thus the task of the cultural historian remains very much the same. He must be able to show in every detail of the period how it reflects its essential economic character.(17, 24)

Lamprecht, whom I mentioned before as one of Warburg's masters, took the opposite line. He looked for the essence not in the material conditions but in the mentality of an age.(68) He tried, in other words, to translate Hegel's *Geist* into psychological terms. The psychology on which he relied, Herbarthian associationism, makes his attempt sound particularly old-fashioned today, but as an effort to rescue or rationalize the Hegelian intuition, his system is still of some interest. A similar turn to psychology was advocated by Wilhelm Dilthey, himself the biographer and a very sophisticated critic of Hegel, who yet, I believe, remained under his spell in the way he posed the problem of what he calls the 'structural unity of culture', especially in his later fragments. He there postulates as 'the most important methodological principle' that a culture should always be approached by the historian 'at its greatest height'.

At this point a state of consciousness has developed in which the relationship of the elements of the culture has found a definite expression in its structure, values, meanings and the sense of life .. which is expressed in ... the configurations of poetry, religion and philosophy. ... The very limitations inherent in any culture even at its height postulate a future. (6, VII, p. 269)

Dilthey is the father of the whole trend of German historiography, significantly called *Geistesgeschichte*, the school which has made it its programme to see art, literature social structure and *Weltanschauung* under the same aspect.(61, 70)

In my own field, the History of Art, it was Alois Riegl who, at the turn of the century, worked out his own translation of the Hegelian system into psychological terms.(57) Like Hegel he saw the evolution of the arts both as an autonomous dialectical process and as wheels revolving within the larger wheel of successive 'world views'. In art the process went spiralling twice: from a tactile mode of apprehension of solid matter to an 'optic' mode, first in the case of isolated objects and then in that of their spatial setting. As in Hegel, also, this process with its inevitable stages puts the idea of 'decline' out of court. By classical standards of tactile clarity the sculpture of the Arch of Constantine may represent a decline, but without this process of dissolution neither Raphael nor Rembrandt could have come into being.

Moreover this relentless development runs parallel with changes in the 'world views' of mankind. Like Hegel, Riegl thought that Egyptian art and Egyptian *Weltanschauung* were both on the opposite pole from 'spiritualism'. He postulates for Egypt a 'materialistic monism' which sees in the soul nothing but refined matter. Greek art and thought are both dualistic while late Antiquity returns to monism, but at the opposite end of the scale, where (predictably) the body is conceived of as a cruder soul.

Anyone who would see in the turn of late antiquity towards irrationalism and magic superstitions a decline, arrogates for himself the right to prescribe to the spirit of mankind the way it should have taken to effect the transition from ancient to modern conceptions. (57, p. 404)

For Riegl was convinced that this late antique belief in spirits and in magic was a necessary stage without which the mind

of man could never have understood electricity (ibid.). And he
proved to his own satisfaction (and to that of many others) that
this momentous process was as clearly manifested in the orna-
mentation of late Roman *fibulae* as it was in the philosophy of
Plotinus.

It was this claim to read the 'signs of the time' and to penetrate into the secrets of the historical process which certainly
gave new impetus to art historical studies. Max Dvořák, in his
later years, represented this trend so perfectly that the editors of
his collected papers rightly chose as their title *Kunstgeschichte
als Geistesgeschichte*(7) ('Art History as a History of the Spirit'),
a formulation which provoked Max J. Friedländer to the quip,
'We apparently are merely studying the History of the Flesh'
('Wir betreiben offenbar nur Körpergeschichte'). The great
Erwin Panofsky, like Dilthey, presents a more critical and
sophisticated development of this programme, but those who
have studied his works know that he too never renounced the
desire to demonstrate the organic unity of all aspects of a
period.(47) His *Gothic Architecture and Scholasticism*(48)
shows him grappling with the attempt to 'rescue' the traditional
connexion between these two aspects of medieval culture by
postulating a 'mental habit' acquired in the schools of the
scholastics and carried over into architectural practice. In his
Renaissance and Renascences in Western Art (49, p. 3) he explicitly defended the notion of cultures having an essence
against the criticism of George Boas.

But perhaps the most original rescue attempt of this kind
was made by the greatest cultural historian after Burckhardt,
his admirer, critic and successor, J. Huizinga.(5, 68)

It will be remembered that Burckhardt had advised his
friend to ask himself: 'How does the spirit of the fifteenth
century express itself in painting?' (3, III, 70)

The average art historian who practised *Geistesgeschichte*

would have started from the impression van Eyck's paintings made on him and proceeded to select other testimonies of the time that appeared to tally with this impression. What is so fascinating in Huizinga is that he took the opposite line. He simply knew too many facts about the age of van Eyck to find it easy to square his impression of his pictures with the voice of the documents. He felt he had rather to re-interpret the style of the painter to make it fit with what he knew of the culture. He did this in his captivating book, *The Waning of the Middle Ages*,(31) literally the autumn of the Middle Ages, which is Hegelian even in the assumption of its title, that here medieval culture had come to its autumnal close, complex, sophisticated and ripe for the sickle. Thus van Eyck's realism could no longer be seen as a harbinger of a new age; his jewel-like richness and his accumulation of detail were rather an expression of the same late Gothic spirit that was also mani-fested much less appealingly in the prolix writings of the period which nobody but specialists read any more.

The wheel had come full circle. The interpretation of artistic realism as an expression of a new spirit, which is to be found in Hegel and which had become the starting point for Burck-ardt's reading of the Renaissance, was effectively questioned by Huizinga who subsequently devoted one of his most searching essays to this traditional equation of Renaissance and Real-ism.(32) But as far as I can see, Huizinga challenged this particu-lar interpretation rather than the methodological assumption according to which the art of an age must be shown to express the same spirit that is expressed by its literature and life.

Critical as he was of all the attempts to establish laws of history, he still ended his wonderful paper on *The Task of Cultural History*(33) with a demand for a 'morphology of cul-ture' that implied, if I understand it correctly, a holistic ap-proach in terms of changing cultural styles.

Now I would not deny for a moment that a great historian such as Huizinga can teach the student of artistic development a lot about the conditions under which a particular style like that of van Eyck took shape. For obviously there is something in the Hegelian intuition that nothing in life is ever isolated, that any event and any creation of a period is connected by a thousand threads with the culture in which it is embedded. Who would not therefore be curious to learn about the life of the patrons who commissioned van Eyck's paintings, about the purpose these paintings served, about the symbolism of his religious paintings, or about the original context of his secular paintings which we only know through copies and reports?

Clearly neither the *Adoration of the Lamb* nor even the lost *Hunt of the Otter* can be understood in isolation without references to religious traditions in the first case and to courtly pastimes in the second.

But is the acknowledgement of this link tantamount to a concession that the Hegelian approach is right after all? I do not think so. It is one thing to see the interconnectedness of things, another to postulate that all aspects of a culture can be traced back to one key cause of which they are the manifestations.(50, 70)

If van Eyck's patrons had all been Buddhists he would neither have painted the *Adoration of the Lamb* nor, for that matter, the *Hunting of the Otter*, but though the fact that he did is therefore trivially connected with the civilization in which he worked, there is no need to place these works on the periphery of the Hegelian wheel and look for the governing cause that explains both otter hunting and piety in the particular form they took in the early decades of the fifteenth century, and which is also expressed in van Eyck's new technique.

If there is one fact in the history of art I do not find very surprising it is the success and acclaim of this novel style. Surely this has less to do with the *Weltanschauung* of the period than with the beauty and sparkle of van Eyck's paintings.

I believe it is one of the undesirable consequences of the Hegelian habit of exegetics that such a remark sounds naïve and even paradoxical. For the habit demands that everything must be treated not only as connected with everything else, but as a symptom of something else. Just as Hegel treated the invention of gunpowder as a necessary expression of the advancing spirit, so the sophisticated historian should treat the invention of oil painting (or what was described as such) as a portent of the times. Why should we not find a simpler explanation in the fact that those who had gunpowder could defeat those who fought with bows and arrows or that those who adopted the van Eyck technique could render light and sparkle better than those who painted in tempera?(20, 23) Of course no such answer is ever final. You are entitled to ask why people wanted to defeat their enemies, and though the question may once have sounded naïve we now know that strong influences can oppose the adoption of a better weapon. We also know that the achievement of life-like illusion cannot always be taken for granted as an aim of painting. It was an aim rejected by Judaism, by Islam, by the Byzantine Church and by our own civilization, in each case for different reasons. I believe indeed that methodologically it is always fruitful to ask for the reasons which made a culture or a society reject a tool or invention which seemed to offer tangible advantages in one particular direction. It is in trying to answer this question that we will discover the reality of that closely knit fabric which we call a culture.(25)

But I see no reason why the study of these connexions should lead us back to the Hegelian postulates of the *Zeitgeist* and *Volksgeist*. On the contrary, I have always believed that it is the exegetic habit of mind leading to these mental short-circuits

which prevents the posing of the very problem Hegelianism
set out to solve.(19, 20)

V. SYMPTOMS AND SYNDROMES

One may be interested in the manifold interactions between
the various spheres of a culture and yet reject what I have called
the 'exegetic method', the method, that is, that bases its inter
pretations on the detection of that kind of 'likeness' that lead
the interpreter of the scriptures to link the passage of the Jew
through the Red Sea with the Baptism of Christ. Hegel, it wi
be remembered, saw in the Egyptian sphinx an essential like
ness with the position of Egyptian culture in which the Spir
began to emerge from animal nature, and carried the sam
metaphor through in his discussion of Egyptian religion an
Egyptian hieroglyphics. The assumption is always that som
essential structural similarity must be detected which permi
the interpreter to subsume the various aspects of a culture und
one formula.(50) The art of van Eyck in Huizinga's persuasiv
morphology is not only to be connected with the theology an
the literature of the time but it must be shown to share som
of their fundamental characteristics. To criticize this assump
tion is not to deny the great ingenuity and learning expende
by some cultural historians on the search for suggestive an
memorable metaphorical descriptions. Nor is it to deny th
such structural likenesses between various aspects of a perio
may be found to be interesting, as A. O. Lovejoy tried
demonstrate for eighteenth-century Deism and Classicism.(3
But here as always any *a priori* assumption of such similari
can only spoil the interest of the search. Not only is there 1
iron law of such isomorphism, I even doubt whether we in
prove matters by replacing this kind of determinism with
probabilistic approach as has been proposed by W. T. Jones

his book on *The Romantic Movement*.(34) The sub-title of this interesting book demands attention by promising a 'new Method in Cultural Anthropology and History of Ideas'; it consists in drawing up such polarities as that between static and dynamic, or order and disorder, and examining certain periods for their bias towards one or the other end of these scales, a bias which would be expected to show up statistically at the periphery of the Hegelian wheel in art, science and political thought, though some of these spheres might be more recalcitrant to their expression than others. In the contrast between 'soft focus' and 'hard focus' the Romantic, he finds, will be likely to lean towards the first in metaphysics, in poetical imagery and in painting, a bias that must be symptomatic of Romantic mentality.

Such expectations, no doubt, accord well with commonsense psychology; but in fact no statistics are needed to show in this case that what looks plausible in this new method of salvaging Hegel still comes into conflict with historical fact. It so happens that it was Romanticism which discovered the taste for the so-called 'primitives' in painting, which meant, at that time, the hard-edged, sharp-focused style of van Eyck or of the early Italians. If the first Romantic painters of Germany had one pet aversion it was the soft-focused bravura of their Baroque predecessors. Whatever their bias in metaphysics may have been, they saw in the smudged outline a symptom of artistic dishonesty and moral corruption. Their bias in the syndrome—to retain this useful term—was based on very different alternatives, alternatives peculiar to the problems of painting. Paradoxically, perhaps, they identified the hard and naïve with the other-worldly and the chaste. It was soft-focused naturalism that was symptomatic of the fall from grace.

We have met this bias before in the discussions among cultural historians of the symptomatic value of painting styles. It might not have assumed such importance if it had not been such a live issue in the very time and ambience of Hegel and of the young Burckhardt. This was of course the time when the trauma of the French Revolution aroused a new longing among certain circles for the lost paradise of medieval culture. The German painters who became known as the Nazarenes regarded realism and sensuality as two inseparable sins and aimed at a linear style redolent of Fra Angelico and his Northern counterparts. They went to Rome where most of them converted to Roman Catholicism, they wore their hair long and walked about in velvet caps considered somehow to be *alt-deutsch* Now here the style of these artists and their *Weltanschauung* was clearly and closely related, their mode of painting, like their costume, was really a badge, a manifesto of their dissociation from the nineteenth century. If you met a member of this circle you could almost infer from his attire what he would say and how he would paint, except, of course, whether he would paint well or badly.

It is legitimate for the cultural historian to ask how such a syndrome arose which marks what we call a movement. It is possible to write the history of such a movement, to speculate about its beginnings and about the reasons for its success or failure. It is equally necessary then to ask how firmly the style and the allegiance it once expressed remained correlated; how long, for instance, the anti-realistic mode of painting remained a badge of Roman Catholicism. In England the link between Catholicism and a love of Gothic is strong in Pugin, but was severed by Ruskin, while the Pre-Raphaelite Brotherhood even aimed at a certain naïve and sharp-focused realism.

Even here, though, the style expressed some kind of allegiance to the Age of Faith. Judging by a passage from Bernard Shaw's first novel, this syndrome had dissolved by 1879 when it was written. In *Immaturity* Shaw wittily described the in terior decoration of a villa belonging to a patron of the arts, a salon with its walls of pale blue damask and its dadoes 'painted with processions of pale maidens, picking flowers to pieces, reading books, looking ecstatically up, looking contemplatively down, playing aborted guitars with an expressive curve of the neck and fingers... all on a ground of dead gold' (pp. 102–3). 'People who disapproved of felt hats, tweed and velveteen clothes, long hair, music on Sundays, pictures of the nude figure, literary women and avowals of agnosticism either dissembled or stayed away.' The syndrome, if Shaw was right, had changed from medievalism to aestheticism and a generalized nonconformism. Burne-Jones was now the badge of allegiance of a progressive creed.

I hope this little example may make it easier to formulate my criticism of Huizinga's Hegelian position *vis-à-vis* van Eyck's realism. For we can now ask with somewhat greater precision whether the style of van Eyck was felt in the Burgundy of his time to belong to any such syndrome, whether, in other words, on entering a great man's hall and finding there a newly acquired painting by the master, you could expect certain other attitudes on the part of your host or his guests. I doubt it. Yet, if this sounds anachronistic, I would venture to suggest that if, only a little later, you had come into a room with a painting of Venus in a style *all'antica* this might have entitled you to expect the owner to want his son to learn good Latin and perhaps, generally, to meet a crowd hoping to discard and transcend the traditions of the past.(23)

VI. MOVEMENTS AND PERIODS

The distinction at which I am aiming here is that between movements and periods. Hegel saw all periods as movements since they were embodiments of the moving spirit. This spirit,

as Hegel taught, manifested itself in a collective, the supra-
individual entities of nations or periods. Since the individual,
in his view, could only be thought of as part of such a collective
it was quite consistent for Hegelians to assume that 'man'
underwent profound changes in the course of history. Nobody
went further in this belief than Oswald Spengler, who assigned
different psyches to his different culture cycles. It was an illusion due to sentimentalizing humanitarians to believe that these
different species of man could ever understand each other.

   The same extremism was of course reflected in the claims of
the totalitarian philosophies which stemmed from Hegel to
create a new 'man', be it of a Soviet or of a National Socialist
variety. Even art historians of a less uncompromising bent
took to speaking of 'Gothic man' or 'Baroque psychology',
assuming a radical change in the mental make-up to have
happened when building firms discarded one pattern book
in favour of another. In fact the study of styles so much fostered
a belief in collective psychology that I remember a discussion
shortly after the war with German students who appeared to
believe that in the Gothic age Gothic cathedrals sprang up
spontaneously all over Europe without any contact between
the building sites.

   It is this belief in the existence of an independent supra-indi-
vidual collective spirit which seems to me to have blocked the
emergence of a true cultural history. I am reminded of certain
recent developments in natural history which may serve as
illustrations. The behaviour of insect colonies appeared to be
so much governed by the needs of the collective that the temptation was great to postulate a super-mind. How else, argued
Marais in his book *The Soul of the White Ant*,(43) could the
individuals of the hive immediately respond to the death of the
queen? The message of this event must reach them through
some kind of telepathic process. We now know that this is not

so. The message is chemical; the queen's substance picked up from her body circulates in the hive through mutual licking rather than through a mysterious mental fluid.(4) Other discoveries about the communication of insects have increased our awareness of the relation between the individual and the hive. We have made progress.

I hope and believe cultural history will make progress if it also fixes its attention firmly on the individual human being. Movements, as distinct from periods, are started by people. Some of them are abortive, others catch on. Each movement in its turn has a core of dedicated souls, a crowd of hangers-on, not to forget a lunatic fringe. There is a whole spectrum of attitudes and degrees of conversion. Even within the individual there may be various levels of conviction, various conscious and unconscious fluctuations in loyalty. What seemed acceptable during the mass rally or revivalist meeting may look pretty crazy on the way home. But movements would not be movements if they did not have their badges, their outward signs, their style of behaviour, style of speech and of dress. Who can probe the motives which prompt individuals to adopt some of these, and who would venture in every case to pronounce on the completeness of the conversion this adoption may express? Knowing these limitations, the cultural historian will be a little wary of the claims of cultural psychology. He will not deny that the success of certain styles may be symptomatic of changing attitudes, but he will resist the temptation to use changing styles and changing fashions as indicators of profound psychological changes. The fact that we cannot assume such automatic connexions makes it more interesting to find out if and when they may have existed.

The Renaissance, for instance, certainly had all the characteristics of a movement. It gradually captured the most articulate sections of society and influenced their attitude in various but

uneven ways. Late Gothic or Mannerism were not, as far as I
can see, the badge of any movement, though of course there
were movements in these periods which may or may not have
been correlated with styles or fashions in other cultural areas.
The great issues of the day, notably the religious movements,
are not necessarily reflected in distinctive styles. Thus both
Mannerism and the Baroque have been claimed to express the
spirit of the Counter-Reformation but neither claim is easy to
substantiate. Even the existence of a peculiar Jesuit style with
propagandist intentions has been disproved by the more detailed
analysis of Francis Haskell.(26)

We need more analyses of this kind based on patient docu-
mentary research, but I venture to suggest that the cultural
historian will want to supplement the analysis of stylistic origins
by an analysis of stylistic associations and responses. Whatever
certain Baroque devices may have meant to their creators, they
evoked Popish associations in the minds of Protestant travellers.
When and where did these associations become conscious? How
far could fashion and the desire for French elegance override
these considerations in a Protestant community? I know that it
is not always easy to answer these questions, but I feel strongly
that it is this type of detailed questioning that should replace
the generalizations of *Geistesgeschichte*.

VII. TOPICS AND TECHNIQUES

The historian does not have to be told that movements offer
promising topics for investigation. The rise of Christianity, of
Puritanism, of the Enlightenment or of Fascism has certainly
not lacked chroniclers in the past and will not lack them in the
future. The very fact that these movements detached themselves from the culture in which they originated offers a principle of selection. But it may be claimed that this advantage is

bought at the expense of offering a panorama of the whole civilization such as Burckhardt or Huizinga tried to offer. The criticism of Hegelian determinism and collectivism therefore strikes indeed at one of the roots of cultural history. But there are other reasons for the malaise of the cultural historian.

The Victorian editor of Cicero's *Letters to Atticus* did not have to subscribe to Hegelian tenets to sketch in what was sometimes called the 'cultural background' in his introduction and notes. He had that unselfconscious sense of continuity with the past that allowed him to take for granted what was in need of explanation, and what was obvious to his readers. The modern student of Cicero's letters has lost this assurance. What is background and what foreground for him in such a cultural document?

But though there is a loss in this uncertainty of perspective, there is also a gain. He will be more aware than his predecessor was of the question he wants to ask. He may search the letters for linguistic, economic, political or psychological evidence, he may be interested in Cicero's attitude to his slaves or his references to his villas. Classical scholars were never debarred from asking this kind of question, but even classics are now threatened by that fragmentation that has long since overtaken the study of later ages.

That same fragmentation also threatens to eliminate another traditional form of cultural history—the old-fashioned biography of the 'Life and Letters' type, which used to present its hero in the living context of his time. I fear, if a survey were made, it would be found that books of this kind are more frequently written nowadays by amateurs than by professional historians. The average academic lacks the nerve to deal with a man of the past who was not also a specialist. Nor is his reluctance dishonourable; we know how little we know about human beings and how little of the evidence we have would satisfy a psychologist interested in the man's character and motives. The increasing awareness of our ignorance about human motives has led to a crisis of self-confidence.

Having criticized a Hegel, a Burckhardt, or a Lamprecht for their excess of self-confidence in trying to solve the riddles of past cultures, I am bound to admit in the end that without confidence our efforts must die of inanition. A scholar such as Warburg would not have founded his Library without a burning faith in the potentialities of *Kulturwissenschaft*. The evolutionist psychology that inspired his faith is no longer ours, but the questions it prompted him to ask still proved fruitful to cultural history. In proposing as the principal theme of his Institute '*das Nachleben der Antike*'—literally the after-life of ancient civilization—he at least made sure that the historian of art, of literature or of science discovered the need for additional techniques to hack a fresh path into the forest in pursuit of that protean problem. Warburg's library was formed precisely to facilitate the acquisition of such tools. It was to encourage trespassing, not amateurishness.

Warburg's problem arose in a situation when the relevance of the classical tradition for the cultural life of the day was increasingly questioned by nationalists and by modernists. He was not out to defend it so much as to explain and assess the reasons for its long 'after-life'. The continued value of that question for the present generation lies in the need to learn more about a once vital tradition which is in danger of being forgotten. But I would not claim that it provides the one privileged entry into the tangled web of Western civilization.

Both the dilemmas and the advantages of cultural history stem from the fact that there can be no privileged entry. It seems to me quite natural that the present generation of students is particularly interested in the social foundations of culture; having myself been born in the reign of his Apostolic Majesty the Emperor Francis Joseph, who had come to the throne in 1848, I certainly can appreciate the rapidity of social change that prompts fresh questionings about the past. That all-pervasive idea of rank and hierarchy that coloured man's reaction to art, religion and even to nature, has become perplexing to the young. It will be the task of the cultural historian to trace and to explain it wherever it is needed for our understanding of the literature, the philosophy or the linguistic conventions of bygone cultures.

Perhaps this example also illustrates the difference between the social and the cultural historian. The first is interested in social change as such. He will use the tools of demography and statistics to map out the transformations in the organization of society. The latter will be grateful for all the information he can glean from such research, but the direction of his interest will still be in the way these changes interacted with other aspects of culture. He will be less interested, for example, in the economic and social causes of urban development than in the changing connotations of words such as 'urbane' or 'suburbia' or, conversely, in the significance of the 'rustic' order in architecture.

The study of such derivations, metaphors and symbols in language, literature and art provides no doubt convenient points of entry into the study of cultural interactions.(70) But I do not think more should be claimed for this approach than it is likely to yield. By itself it cannot offer an escape from the basic dilemma caused by the breakdown of the Hegelian tradition, which stems from the chastening insight that no culture can be mapped out in its entirety, but no element of this culture can be understood in isolation. It appears as if the cultural historian were thus still left without a viable programme, grubbing among the random curiosities of antiquarian lore.

I realize that this perplexity looks pretty formidable in the

"my teacher" will bow to W. Webster.

abstract, but I believe it is much less discouraging in practice. What Popper has stressed for the scientist also applies to the scholar.(55) No cultural historian ever starts from scratch. The traditions of his own culture, the bias of his teacher, the questions of the moment can all stimulate his curiosity and direct his questionings. He may want to continue some existing lines of research or to challenge their result; he may be captivated by Burckhardt's picture of the Renaissance, for instance, and fill in some of the gaps left in that immensely suggestive account, or he may have come to distrust its theoretical scaffolding and therefore feel prompted to ask how far and by whom certain Neo-Platonic tenets were accepted as an alternative to the Christian dogma.

Whether we know it or not, we always approach the past with some preconceived ideas, with a rudimentary theory we wish to test. In this as in many other respects the cultural historian does not differ all that much from his predecessor, the traveller to foreign lands. Not the professional traveller who is only interested in one particular errand, be it the exploration of a country's kinship system or its hydro-electric schemes, but the broadminded traveller who wants to understand the culture of the country in which he finds himself.

In trying to widen his understanding the traveller will always be well advised to treat inherited clichés about national characters or social types with a healthy suspicion, just as the cultural historian will distrust the second-hand stereotypes of the 'spirit of the age'. But neither need we ever forget that our reactions and observations will always be dependent on the initial assumptions with which we approach a foreign civilization. The questions we may wish to ask are therefore in no way random; they are related to a whole body of beliefs we wish to reinforce or to challenge. But for the cultural historian no less than for the traveller the formulation of the question will

the use of the word "picturesque"
as a positive term, e.g., in the
Times supplement.

or different uses
of different
sources.

usually be precipitated by an individual encounter, a striking
instance, be it a work of art or a puzzling custom, a strange
craft, or a conversation in a minicab.

Take any letter that arouses our attention, say Burckhardt's
letter to Fresenius on Hegel to which I have referred. Clearly
we may use it as a document for a study of Burckhardt and his
circle of friends, and try to build up, through careful reading
and an expansion of the references, a picture of that 'subculture'
in which the young Burckhardt moved. But we can also change
the focus and use the letter as a starting point for very different
lines of research—for instance into the history of epistolary
styles. A hundred years earlier a student would have been most
unlikely to pour this kind of confession into a letter to a friend,
and if we go back to the Renaissance such a self-revelation, for
which there is no Ciceronian model, would have been unthink-
able. We might of course shift the focus even further and ask
about the history of forms of address; we may wonder whether
Burckhardt wrote with a quill and when this habit came to
an end. We may speculate about the influence of postal services
on the form of communications and blame the telephone for
the relative decline of letter-writing today. By and large, therefore, we may either be interested in individuals and the situation they found themselves in, or in traditions passed on by
hosts of anonymous people. If labels are needed we may speak
of contiguity and continuity studies, though neither of these
can be kept wholly apart from the other. The research into
continuities may lead us still to individuals who stand out of
the anonymous crowd for the impact they made on traditions,
and the biographical approach will raise ever fresh questions
about cultural conventions, their origins, and the time of their
validity.

Either approach may thus lead us to consult works on
economics or social science, on psychology or on the theory of

communication; unless we do, we risk talking nonsense, but for
the question in hand theories are critical tools rather than ends
in themselves. It is true that the cultural historian may harbour
ulterior ambitions; he sometimes dares to hope that there is a
bonus in store for good work in this as in any other field. A
worth-while contribution to cultural history may transcend the
particular, suggesting to other students of culture fresh ideas
about the innumerable ways various aspects of a civilization can
interact.

Of these interactions, the way forms, symbols and words
become charged with what might be called cultural meanings
seems to me to offer a particular challenge to the cultural historian. I have tried to hint at this problem at the outset of this
lecture in drawing attention to certain overtones of the word
'culture' which can hardly be found in any dictionary. In our
own cultural environment we catch these resonances without
having to spell them out; the picture on the wall of the living-
room, the accent, the handwriting, the manner of dress and
the manner of greeting all reverberate for us with countless
such cultural and social overtones, but if we are no Hegelians
we also realize that these clusters of meaning cannot always be
interpreted correctly in psychological terms. Much criticism of
contemporary culture by the elderly misses the mark for this
very reason. The widespread success of so-called psychedelic
patterns is not really correlated to the strength of this silly and
suicidal cult, but it still mildly partakes of the flavour of
escapist conformism, which is not, I hope, a portent of things
to come. It is only the Hegelian who believes that whatever is
is right and who therefore has no intellectual defences against
the self-appointed spokesman of the *Zeitgeist*.

I have alluded to styles in painting, in dress and in pattern-
making, but the best example of what I mean by resonance is
surely the realm of music. The jazzy rhythm, the folksy tune,

the march, the hymn, the minuet, they all evoke clusters of cultural resonances which we do not have to have explained.

Or do we? I think my own roots are still sufficiently deep in the past for me to understand Beethoven's Pastoral Symphony. I do not claim that I have ever seen merry-making peasants quite in the style Beethoven saw, or that I have joined in a Thanksgiving hymn after a thunderstorm, but all these associations still come naturally to me as I can connect the 'awakening of cheerful emotions on arrival in the country' with my own memory of excursions from Vienna.

But today you leave the city by car along a motor-road which leads through ribbon developments to petrol stations. There are no merry-making peasants either in life or even in fiction, and attendance at Thanksgiving services is notoriously small. The mood of the 'pastoral' may soon have to be explained as elaborately as has the mood or 'flavour' of an Indian Raga.

Our own past is moving away from us at frightening speed, and if we want to keep open the lines of communication which permit us to understand the greatest creations of mankind we must study and teach the history of culture more deeply and more intensely than was necessary a generation ago, when many more of such resonances were still to be expected as a matter of course. If cultural history did not exist, it would have to be invented now.

VIII. ACADEMIC ATTITUDES

It seems to me that the academic world is very slow indeed in responding to this growing need. History in our universities still means largely political and perhaps economic history. It is true that a few other disciplines have also by now received a licence to make their own cuttings into the forest of the past in pursuit of the history of literature, of music, of art, or of science. But unless I am much mistaken students are frequently advised to keep to these straight and narrow paths to the Finals and onwards to research, looking neither right nor left and leaving vast areas of the forest unvisited and unexplored.

I would hate the idea of my criticism of *Geistesgeschichte* giving aid and comfort to such enemies of cultural history. It cannot be repeated sufficiently often that the so-called 'disciplines' on which our academic organization is founded are no more than techniques; they are means to an end but no more than that. Clearly the historian of music must learn to read scores, and the economic historian must be able to handle statistics. But it will be a sad day when we allow the techniques we have learned or which we teach to dictate the questions which can be asked in our universities.

If the cultural historian lacks a voice in academic councils, it is because he does not represent a technique, a discipline. Yet I do not think he should emulate his colleagues from the departments of sociology in staking a claim to a method and terminology of his own.(63) For whatever he may be able to learn from this and other approaches to the study of civilizations and societies, his concern, I believe, should still be with the individual and particular rather than with that study of structures and patterns which is rarely free of Hegelian holism.(53, 65) For that same reason I would not want him to compete for the cacophonic label of an interdisciplinary discipline, for this claim implies the belief in the Hegelian wheel and in the need to survey the apparently God-given separate aspects of a culture from one privileged centre. It was the purpose of this paper to suggest that this Hegelian wheel is really a secularized diagram of the Divine plan; the search for a centre that determines the total pattern of a civilization is consequently no more, but also no less, than the quest for an initiation into God's ways with man. But I hope I have also made it clear why the disappoint-

interdisciplinary awareness needed. but this leads to no ultimate, comprehensive truths about culture.

ing truth that we cannot be omniscient must on no account lead us to the adoption of an attitude of blinkered ignorance. We simply cannot afford this degree of professionalization if the humanities are to survive at all.

I know that sermons against specialization are two a penny and that they are unlikely to make an impression on those who know how hard it is even to master a small field of research. But I should like to urge here the essential difference, in this respect, between the role of research in the sciences and in the humanities. The scientist, if I understand the situation, must always work on the frontiers of knowledge. He must therefore select a small sector in which hypotheses can be tested and revised by means of experiments which may be costly and time-consuming. He, too, no doubt, should be able to survey a larger field, and be well-read in the neighbouring disciplines, but what he is ultimately valued for is his discoveries rather than his knowledge. It is different, I contend, with the humanist. Humanistic education aims first and foremost at knowledge, that knowledge that used to be called 'culture'.(21) In the past this culture was largely transmitted and absorbed in the home or on travels. The universities did not concern themselves with such subjects as history or literature, art or music. Their aim was mainly vocational, and even a training in the Classics, though valued by society, had its vocational reasons. Nobody thought that it was the purpose of a university education to tell students about Shakespeare or Dickens, Michelangelo or Bach. These were things the 'cultured' person knew. They were neither fit objects for examinations nor for research. I happen to have some sympathy for this old-fashioned approach, for I think that the humanist really differs from the scientist in his relative valuation of knowledge and research. It is more relevant to know Shakespeare, or Michelangelo than to 'do research' about them. Research may yield nothing fresh, but knowledge yields pleasure and enrichment. It seems a thousand pities that our universities are so organized that this difference is not acknowledged. Much of the malaise of the humanities might disappear overnight if it became clear that they need not ape the sciences in order to remain respectable. There may be a science of culture, but this belongs to anthropology and sociology. The cultural historian wants to be a scholar, not a scientist. He wants to give his students and his readers access to the creations of other minds; research, here, is incidental. Not that it is never necessary. We may suspect current interpretations of Shakespeare or the way Bach is performed and want to get at the truth of the matter. But in all this research the cultural historian really aims at serving culture rather than at feeding the academic industry.

This industry, I fear, threatens to become an enemy of culture and of cultural history. Few people can read and write at the same time; and while we pursue our major and minor problems of research, the unread masterpieces of the past look at us reproachfully from the shelves.

But who, today, still feels this reproach? In our world it is the phrase 'a cloistered scholar' that reverberates with reproach. The cultural historian draws his salary from the taxpayer and should serve him as best he can.

I hope I have made it clear in what his service can consist. For good or ill the universities have taken over from the home much of the function of transmitting the values of our civilization. We cannot expect them to get more thanks for this from some of the students than the parental home sometimes got in the past. We surely want these values to be probed and scrutinized, but to do so effectively their critics must know them. Hence I do not see why we should feel apologetic towards those who urge us to concern ourselves with the present rather than with the past. The study of culture is largely the study of continuities, and it is this sense of continuity rather than of uncritical acceptance we hope to impart to our students. We want them to acquire a habit of mind that looks for these continuities not only within the confines of their special field, but in all the manifestations of culture that surround them.

Take the occasion of this paper. When I was honoured by the invitation to give the Philip Maurice Deneke Lecture, the question naturally struck me how the Institution arose in which I was to play a part. I knew that this particular series owes its existence to the beneficence of the Misses Deneke who instituted it in 1931 in memory of their father. But in making this benefaction they followed a tradition which is by now firmly established in the whole Anglo-Saxon world, the tradition of named lectures as monuments to private persons.

It took a 'traveller from foreign lands' to notice this tradition, for I found that my English colleagues took it so much for granted that I had to explain and confirm that there are no such lectures on the continent of Europe.

In England, it turned out, these lectureships developed organically out of the educational foundations exemplified by the colleges of the ancient universities which, in their turn, arose quite naturally from the medieval bequests for chantries. France still witnessed a parallel growth in the Sorbonne of Paris, called after a private founder, but soon the privilege of naming such institutions was apparently confined to princes and rulers. My own school in Vienna was called the Theresianum, after the Empress, but not before the nineteenth century were Austrian schools called after commoners. What was it that secured this continuity and ramification in England? What induced Lady Margaret Beaufort to found a Lady Margaret Readership and what part was played in the encouragement and preservation of this swelling number of benefactions by the Laws of Trust which are also apparently peculiar to this country?(35) Admittedly I found it safer to ask these questions at the end of this paper rather than at the beginning, for I do not know the answers. But I believe that these answers could be found and that they need be neither vague nor, as the jargon has it, 'value free'. Paying tribute to a great tradition, they would also help to vindicate the name and function of cultural history.

Bibliography

1. Jacques Barzun, 'Cultural History as a Synthesis', *The Varieties of History*, ed. Fritz Stern, 1956, pp. 387–402.

2. Jacob Burckhardt, *Gesamtausgabe*, Berlin and Leipzig, 1930 et seq.

3. — *Briefe*, vollständige Ausgabe, ed. Max Burckhardt, Basel, 1949 et seq.

4. Colin G. Butler, *The World of the Honeybee*, London, 1954.

5. R. L. Colie, 'John Huizinga and the Task of Cultural History', *American Historical Review*, lxix (1964), pp. 607–30.

6. Wilhelm Dilthey, *Der Aufbau der geschichtlichen Welt in der Geisteswissenschaft* (Plan und Fortsetzung). Gesammelte Schriften, VII, Leipzig und Berlin, 1927.

7. Max Dvořák, *Kunstgeschichte als Geistesgeschichte*, Munich, 1924.

8. T. S. Eliot, *Notes towards the Definition of Culture*, London, 1948.

9. Emil Fackenheim, *The Religious Dimension in Hegel's Thought*, Bloomington, 1967.

10. W. K. Fergusson, *The Renaissance in Historical Thought*, Cambridge, Mass., 1948.

11. J. N. Findlay, *Hegel: A Re-Examination*, London, 1958.

12. L. Fox (ed.), *English Historical Scholarship in the 16th and 17th Century*, Oxford, 1956.

13. A. Funkenstein, *Heilsplan und natürliche Entwicklung, Formen der Gegenwartsbestimmung im Geschichtsdenken des hohen Mittelalters*, Munich, 1965.

14. Leona Gabel *et. al.*, 'The Renaissance Reconsidered', A Symposium, *Smith College Studies in History*, XLIV, 1964, Northampton, Mass.

15. Felix Gilbert, 'Cultural History and Its Problems', *Comité International des Sciences Historiques*, Rapports, 1960, vol. i, pp. 40–58.

16. Carlo Ginzburg, 'Da A. Warburg a E. H. Gombrich (Note su un Problema di Metodo)', *Studi Medievali*, S. III, 7, 1966.

17. E. H. Gombrich, 'The Social History of Art' (1953), *Meditations on a Hobby Horse*, London, 1963.

18. — 'Renaissance and Golden Age' (1955), *Norm and Form*, London, 1966.

19. — 'Art and Scholarship' (1957), *Meditations on a Hobby Horse*, London, 1963.

20. — *Art and Illusion*, New York and London, 1960.

21. — 'The Tradition of General Knowledge' (1961), M. Bunge (ed.), *The Critical Approach to Science and Philosophy*, New York, 1964.

22. — 'Aby Warburg zum Gedenken', *Jahrbuch der Hamburger Kunstsammlungen*, xi, 1966.

23. — 'From the Revival of Letters to the Reform of the Arts: Niccolò Niccoli and Filippo Brunelleschi', *Essays in the History of Art presented to Rudolf Wittkower* (ed. D. A. Fraser *et al.*), London, 1967.

24. — 'Style', *International Encyclopedia of the Social Sciences*, New York, 1968.

25. — 'The Logic of Vanity Fair, Alternatives to Historicism in the Study of Fashions, Style and Taste', to be published in *The Philosophy of K. R. Popper* (The Library of Living Philosophers, ed. P. A. Schilpp).

26. Francis Haskell, *Patrons and Painters*, London, 1963.

27. Georg Wilhelm Friedrich Hegel, 'Vorlesungen über die Philosophie der Religion', II, *Sämtliche Werke*, XVI.

28. — 'Vom göttlichen Dreieck', *Dokumente zu Hegels Entwicklung*, ed. J. Hoffmeister, Stuttgart, 1936, pp. 303–6.

29. — 'Vorlesungen über die Philosophie der Geschichte', *Sämtliche Werke*, ed. H. Glockner, XI, Stuttgart, 1928.

30. Tinsley Helton (ed.), *The Renaissance, a Reconsideration of the Theories and Interpretations of the Age*, Madison, 1961.

31. J. Huizinga, *The Waning of the Middle Ages* (1919), London, 1924.

32. — 'Renaissance and Realism' (1926), *Men and Ideas*, New York, 1959.

33. — 'The Task of Cultural History' (1929), *Men and Ideas*, New York, 1959.

34. W. T. Jones, *The Romantic Syndrome*, The Hague, 1961.

35. W. K. Jordan, *Philanthropy in England, 1480–1660*, London, 1959.

36. Werner Kaegi, *Jacob Burckhardt*, III, Basel-Stuttgart, 1956.

37. A. L. Kroeber and Clyde Kluckhohn, *Culture, a Critical Review of Concepts and Definitions*, New York, 1963.

38. Harry Levin, 'Semantics of Culture', *Science and Culture*, *Daedalus*, Winter, 1965.

39. A. O. Lovejoy, 'The Parallel between Deism and Classicism', *Essays in the History of Ideas*, Baltimore, 1948.

40. K. Löwith, *Jacob Burckhardt, der Mensch inmitten der Geschichte*, Luzern, 1936.

41. Thomas Mann, *Friedrich und die große Koalition*, Berlin, 1915.

42. Frank E. Manuel, *Shapes of Philosophical History*, Stanford, 1965.

43. Eugene Marais, *The Soul of the White Ant* (1934), London, 1937.

44. Bruce Mazlish, *The Riddle of History: The Great Speculators from Vico to Freud*, New York and London, 1966.

45. Arnaldo Momigliano, 'Ancient History and the Antiquarian', *Journal of the Warburg and Courtauld Institutes*, xiii (1950), pp 285–315.

46. — 'Introduzione alla Griechische Kulturgeschichte di Jacob Burckhardt', *Secondo Contributo alla Storia degli Studi Classici*, Rome, 1960, pp. 283–98. (With an important bibliographical appendix on Burckhardt up to 1959.)

47. E. Panofsky, *Aufsätze zu Grundfragen der Kunstwissenschaft*, Berlin, 1964.

48. — *Gothic Architecture and Scholasticism*, Latrobe, Pa., 1951.

49. — *Renaissance and Renascences in Western Art*, Stockholm, 1960.

50. Morse Peckham, *Man's Rush for Chaos*, New York, 1966.

51. G. M. Pflaum, *Geschichte des Wortes 'Zivilisation'*, Dissertation, University of Munich, 1961. (Copy at the Warburg Institute.)

52. K. R. Popper, 'What is Dialectic?' (1940), *Conjectures and Refutations*, London, 1963.

53. — *The Poverty of Historicism* (1944), London, 1957.

54. — *The Open Society and its Enemies* (1946), London, 1966.

55. — 'Truth, Rationality and the Growth of Scientific Knowledge' (1960), *Conjectures and Refutations*, London, 1963.

56. F. Rauhut, 'Die Herkunft der Worte und Begriffe "Kultur", "Zivilisation" und "Bildung",' *Germanisch-Romanische Monatschrift*, Neue Folge, 1953, 3, 1, pp. 81–91.

57. Alois Riegl, *Die Spätrömische Kunstindustrie* (1901), Vienna, 1927.

58. Gerhard Ritter, 'Zum Begriff der Kulturgeschichte', *Historische Zeitschrift* 171, 1951, pp. 293–302.

59. Bertrand Russell, *History of Western Philosophy*, London, 1946.

60. Carl Schnaase, *Geschichte der bildenden Künste*, I, Leipzig, 1843.

61. Hans-Joachim Schoeps, *Was ist und was will die Geistesgeschichte? Über die Theorie und Praxis der Zeitgeistforschung*, Göttingen, 1959.

62. Milton Singer, 'Culture (Concept)', *International Encyclopedia of the Social Sciences*, New York, 1968.

63. N. Timasheff, *Sociological Theory*, New York, 1967.

64. Ernest Lee Tuveson, *Millenium and Utopia, a Study in the Background of the Idea of Progress*, Berkeley and Los Angeles, 1949.

65. Evon Z. Vogt, 'Culture Change', *International Encyclopedia of the Social Sciences*, New York, 1968.

66. Galvano della Volpe, *Hegel, Romantico e Mistico*, Florence, 1929.

67. Joachim Wach, *Das Verstehen*, Tübingen, 1926–33.

68. Karl J. Weintraub, *Visions of Culture*, Chicago and London, 1966.

69. Raymond Williams, *Culture and Society 1780–1950*, London, 1958.

70. Edgar Wind, 'Kritik der Geistesgeschichte, Das Symbol als Gegenstand Kulturwissenschaftlicher Forschung', *Kulturwissenschaftliche Bibliographie zum Nachleben der Antike*, Einleitung, ed. Bibliothek Warburg, I, Leipzig, Berlin, 1934.

71. H. Wölfflin, *Renaissance und Barock*, Munich, 1888.